Winded from the Chase

Winded from the Chase

Poems by

Linda Malm

Cover design by Shay Culligan
Cover digital image "Train Girl" by Charles Kohlhase
http://charleysorbitusa.com
Author's photo by Karen Young

ISBN: 978-1-63980-288-3

Kelsay Books
502 South 1040 East, A-119
American Fork, Utah 84003
Kelsaybooks.com

For Sawnie Morris

Three blue flower pillows
torn from their mooring
skip through the air—

Acknowledgments

Thank you to the following journals, which published versions of these poems:

Abandoned Mine: "Foxes"

Adobe Walls: An Anthology of New Mexico Poetry #4: "Garden Snake"

Smoky Blue Literary and Arts Magazine: "I Need"

Taos Journal of Poetry: "Kairos"

Ubu. Small Absurdist Poems #5: "Clay" (excerpt)

Waywords #9: "The Scale of Things"

Contents

Artist's Statement

I find being a poet is about seeing and then re-imagining the original image. Sometimes linear language can assume other dimensions that surprise both the poet and reader. "To Dare One's Ghosts" is a collage of all the poems that follow. "Crow Familiar" can be read down or across columns. Some other poems in this collection make internal leaps. Often a risk with accessibility is a gain in play and complexity. The craft of working with language and form hones the poem. Often a new speaker emerges. The poem becomes its own.

To Dare One's Ghosts

Cast blue shreds into the future. Create a more welcoming time.

My white clematis blooms look like crumpled papers, revisions
on each page.

A gift from a snake—gray lace, stripes and stipples—
lies across sheaves of my dark words.

Sometimes a man enters my writing space. A burst of heat,
the low wind-sound a fire makes.

Merwin said he only had what he remembered.

It gives meaning to where we are. Shadows talk. Books, like trees,
hold time.

*

If you asked me the cost of life I've given to be with this land,
I'd say it was fair.

Deserts bloom quick as the flick of a rattlesnake's tongue.

There are rivers and seas, peaks and plains, palo verde, palmettos
and pines.

Mud is alive. I cup it in both hands.

Daylight slants. Stars have veered according to the season.

What am I but autumn passing? In too few days bees complete
their golden pollen-sweeps. Petals crinkle brown.

Shadows lurk, blacken the sand. Old age comes with force
and fascination.

Oh! A yellow leaf catches in my gray blown hair.

*

My voice rises free as milkweed seed playing the breeze.
Chorusing robins scatter.

Beneath toothed leaves, white horns splay.

Camouflaged music, bee and hummingbird resonant wings.

A cello draws a disquieting tone; there is more than one rhythm.

I make a flute, blow through the hollow wing bone, a lyrical river.

My blue dance dress is silk. The hem ripples.

*

I stroke my bird's soft breast feathers. Fra Angelico's pale idea
of angel.

Her strong wings spread, bank and veer.

My wild familiar cuts into wind, slices cloudless sky until a dot.

My lost spirit-lifter. What else but love comforts grief.

The price for stewardship was fair.

*

If you ask what makes me most afraid, which lie would I tell?

If I came face to face with the bear, her hunger, our fear—
fluttering shirt, ruffled up fur—

I'd stand still, pretend to be big.

A statuesque woman—sinewy arms, strong thighs, wavy hair.

Comic or fierce?

I scumble and layer. Ride fear like a fast horse.

*

I allow myself a more feral mind: a furtive slink, a glimpse of lope.

I already feel among them. We share magna-warmed water.

I'll wear a mask—my own carved face, goat horns, fanged teeth
and silly splayed animal ears.

I seek to know my animal. What angel heralds the vision quest?

Each spirit-wish and fear confronted

I shed old skin whole, leave past ghosts to gravel.

*

Out on a crumbing jetty a man is scaling a silver fish.

An iridescent fly, the flycatcher's ease.

A murder of crows assails a rare solitary hawk.

Coyotes howl hunger across arid arroyos. Diminishing rabbits
renew each year.

I'm awed that everything barbed survives being eaten, bitten
or gnawed.

Always this living with dying.

*

A meteor at light-year's end engraves a burning arc into the hill.

Saturn rolls toward me, rock and ice rings wheeling like birds.

I create mythology from pinpoints of light to reckon vastness.
It scales down self-importance to me, not unlike praying.

Nebula mesh like clouds of snow—stars and space fold
into each other.

I mix the stars deep in my mind for dreaming.

I am stardust in motion.

Swirl

I buy a Gulah-Geechee sweetgrass basket. The vendor tells me
it is woven alive from palmetto and pine.

Pavement rings palmettos and pines. Condominium shadows
blacken the sand, drive me toward sun still on the shore.

Pelicans veer past blank balconies. Iceberg ships cruise out
  from the bay. Dolphin speech-bubbles cry. Sewage and blades.

I trail through warm fingers of foam, while putty clouds roil
and the sea gloss fades.

A rapid tide swells. A row of red trucks continue to dump sand
  in a kind of child's play.

Out on the crumbling jetty a man is scaling a silver fish.

On the new storm wall, a statuesque woman appears by a bench
  wavy wild hair, sequined dress.

She places a cello between her strong thighs, a sinewy arm slides
  a long bow, draws a disquieting tone.

The sea is counterpoint musicality.

I find a swirled conch shell; pry open my basket to put it in.
  Decipher the storm eye calmly centered in coils.

Mask

We have walked under the folk-devil festival mask
hanging above the restaurant door—a carved human face,
goat horns and silly splayed animal ears, once painted black.
White slanted eyes and prominent pupils scrutinize.

The close seating feels like I'm sharing a
neighborhood meal. Only the music makes space.
The country of Willy and Waylon plays over the
air-cooler hiss. Back in the hot kitchen mariachi competes.

The mask has a broad flared nose and fanged animal teeth.
An old cowboy marvels that this morning he touched
something cold then saw a diamond-back snake. He shoves
up his hat. Smoke from his cigarette floats in his face.

The skinny blonde laughs. Her tight pants have rhinestone
trim. She leans into him, asks for a drag in a low raspy voice.
He slides the cigarette from between his dry lips. The mask
has a long leather tongue stuck out with jaw-dropping force

that furrows its forehead and hollows its cheeks. I can't tell
if it's comic or fierce, a growl or response to a rancid taste.
A tattooed teen has burrowed his body in a baggy T-shirt
over low-crotched jeans. (He has room for a gun down his leg.)

My horoscope says the moon is in Libra: *The tension
of maintaining balance has you on edge.*
I need to put on the mask,
                    learn to wear fun and fear lightly.

The Old Days, Many Now Dead

Once I made a lucky jump onto an interested body.
Both of us amazed. We lathered each other in soap suds.
Laughed in anticipation. Stripped satin sheets
with our bodies until the mattress was bare.
Very far from tantric.

You/we made love not long after I buried my dad.
What else but love comforts grief?

Outside it was wolf whistles, babes and chicks.
Once in Italy, a row of men lounged on a wall,
each rhythmically stroking his crotch as I passed.
I could not pass by my boss's awkward lunge, even with
counterfeit giggles, the ruse of *but I have a boyfriend.*

My fast forearms warded off touching belly to belly.

A pro bono offer of help wasn't free.

There was danger of drugs in the drinks of the unwilling.

Promotion denied. I quit.

The Love Poem Is Back

And when he asked if I'd shave his back I stripped
to my underwear

while he stood naked in the shower, athletic, back side out,
while he stood with razors waiting with the water off

ready for the operation. I call the electric razor brush-hog,
the manual one is for serious detailed work.

I clasp the curve of his perfect shoulder as I buzz down his back.
As I buzz, he stretches skin taught.

Halfway silly, I halfway sing—birds do it, monkeys do it—
Let's preen—let's fall . . .

Familiar topography: one or two warts, scar patch, three moles,
something harmless that looks like a tiny volcano.

Shearing, followed by more watchful blade work.

I call this grooming, not the vigilant search for recurrent
melanoma, the suspicious change in a mole or uneven dark mark.

I finish the shave at the base of his spine. Relieved.
Medically done. I Mae-West-murmur *Great butt.*

I kiss it like I would a baby's,

kiss it like I love to kiss him   *oh baby.*

He indulges me. *Thanks*, with a bit of finality, then turns on
the water.   He turns in sweet water.

I Need

I have a need for resilience. Granite peaks thrust through
the desert, rusted volcanics accrete. Tectonic turmoil revealed
in escarpments. I read earth's past in a geological frieze. Eons
of storm winds grind mountains to gravel. My alluvial fan flows
into the plain. I don't need a gated community, fountains on
manicured grounds. I drink deep magna-warmed water.

I have a need.

I must have a garden, although I no longer can get up from worn
knees. I water wild bushes to quicken their lifetime to mine.
I am awed by wild plant survival—cactus, yucca, mesquite
strategies. Roots tap deep or spread wide, sprout resilient spines
and curled or thick leaves. Wild poppies flare briefly, then the long
wait of their far-flung seeds. I borrow this garden.

I have a need.

This latitude tempers the winter and seems to lengthen the days
that end in the splendor of sunsets—plums, roses, citrus blaze.
Nights reveal patterns of light, some can imagine mythologies.
This celestial clock only seems to circle our planet.
I've studied the stars.
The vastness scales down self-importance for me.

I have this need.

I welcome hesitant deer and skittery coveys of quail. I witness
wildlife ferocities—the iridescent fly, the flycatcher's ease.
Moonlight casts feral shadows: a furtive slink, a glimpse of lope.
Coyotes howl hunger across the arid arroyos. Diminished rabbits
renew each year. Always this living with dying.

I have a need.

Chance

The museum guard lends me a hand checking my winter coat.
A live exhibition of butterfly snowflakes fills the humid
vast room. A varied blue chooses my hand. Flutters there.
A golden stipple weightlessly rests in my hair.

I come to pick the flushed cherry tree. Chorusing robins
disrupted. I give a flamboyant toast: undertones of red plum
and rich earthy leather. A ruby throated hummingbird
persistently hovers over my red shirted breast. I mimic its thrum.

If you asked what makes me most afraid, which lie would I tell
you or myself? I scumble and layer. Seek truth lying under
tough skin. Feminists speak: *feel the fear and do it anyway;*
a famous fighter declared: *I ride my fear like a fast horse.*

I speed down the River Gorge trail. I could fall far enough
to fear. The horizon recedes. It is spiritual here. Snow curds
float the river like the fluffy free cake on the entry table at the
Buffalo Thunder Casino. In games of chance, I could only lose.

In a sunny field a child builds a snowman. Brief childhood,
briefer snowman. In time the carrot nose drops, the exuberant
stick arms fall. He leans toward the woods. Strong cinder eyes
and broad smile are the last to go. Scattered in snowman remains.

My breaths are a burst of heat with the low wind sound
a fire makes. I stumble crossing a stream, dislodge a stone,
change the waters' cadence. A confusion of currents swirl,
as if they could choose a different direction.

Foxes

After we have amicably divided your possessions,
a fox, timid and intent, stands at the far edge of your garden,
stares at me musing in your rocker by the open slider door.
I didn't know of foxes in your forest,
but there in dappled light her coat shone
the color of your hair remembered from my childhood,
then she turned and vanished into your beloved woods

where you had made me feel the earth and swear I'd leave
you where wild roots would pull your body's ashes in.
    The rocks I pile to mark this place, your den.

Where I'm @

I press my chest into the sunny grass and sob into warm earth.
My dog was killed on my husband's watch. We can't rub
her shadow off the floor.

There is a sweet layer between ripe wild grape skin and seeds.
The globby center is tart. I swallow the sweet
and spit out the bitter; the more explosive, the better.

I leave him for a landscape of camouflaged music.
My voice rises free as milkweed seed. Ripened
and playing the breeze.

A hunting hawk spirals above me, an arrow of migrating
geese aims for the marsh low on the horizon.
I see there is more than one rhythm.

Butterflies cluster, fold wings to drink on a patch of damp
sand. I move closer. Triangles open, sulfur flakes flutter.
Sometimes a man enters my writing space.

Clematis blooms look like my crumpled white paper
caught in the vines. I use a sharp yellow pencil
to squeeze in revisions on a typed page.

A woman leans into her walker, someone holds her mike.
She recites the best poems she has ever written.
Then with help, she rolls past the band.

Goodbye.
         She stops to sign one last book.
                              I am happy for her.

Libraries

I.

At the children's' library opening, mother tugged my hand.
She wanted me to meet the dedication speaker, Eleanor Roosevelt.
Attention is love. Mother was full of dreams.

My first view of art was the library frieze—like a wild Pollock.
The building had peaked skylights, low blond-wood cases
brimming with books, and a reading garden.

I would get caught in a book when I curled in the cowhide
sling chairs. I looked at the card in the front cover pocket
for the names of those who had read it before.

Amazon used books regularly arrive. Some have comments
or names. Merwin touched my copy of *The Shadow of Sirius*.
He had signed it and added a drawing of a dog' paw.

Sirius is the brightest star, a radio network, a car, a ship
and more. Merwin said he had only what he remembers.
Mount Monadnock is always on the horizon, a lone granite peak.

The newspaper headline announced: *A boy caught a trout!*
The town's industrial base had eroded.
The river recovered from silt.

I want to rejuvenate the youth library: bring back children's
shushed voices, the beauty of lean design. Water stains
streak the peaked skylights. The reading garden is dry.

The great Alexandrian library declined years before
it burned (nine muses couldn't fund it).
World scholars decried.

My first adult library had translucent glass floors that illuminated
lower stacks. I read the long shelf on nature. The card catalogues
that lined the main room promised more.

At my collage library I achieved my mother's ambition:
I met a professional man and left the hometown. I didn't
know one could listen and still resist. I married. It failed.

I saw advice on a Chinese placemat: *You are a Zodiac dragon.*
Marry a monkey or rat. Avoid a . . . Yes, I am a dragon. Where
is the balance between social disguise and authentic self?

The Boston Public Library reading rooms were a safe place
to isolate when I was sad. They were quiet and spacious
with carved coffered ceilings and warm yellow light.

I was awed by the archives at UCLA; an Alexandrian
holding of all the world's words. Some stacks were dark, with
mesh-metal floors for circulating air and preventing worms.

Perhaps I admire libraries because it's so hard to write.
I search for a snack, take breaks to dead-head my flowers.
Approach the computer again.

II.

It is useful to write stories of my past. I cast them into
the future to create a more welcoming time.
I allow myself a more feral mind.

If you want something you have never had you must do
something you've never done. When I select books for
my class I pick wise creature stories—not fairy tales.

For the library nook I choose soft carpet. Each child
wants to touch me when I read aloud. I sit on the floor
and make my legs long.

III.

It matters what meaning you make of where you are. Now
I live in volcanic wilderness mountains—granite below. I read
stars. Sirius is faithfully present in the dog constellation.

I commission a granite bench to identify two unmarked graves.
It is inscribed with Mom and Dad's dates—actually it says
in "memory" of mother, who is not buried there.

Her ashes are scattered at sea. She always insisted
she would get out of our town. The bench shows my sister's
and my birthdates, each followed by a short dash.

In Spring, blue forget-me-nots bloom there. A Veteran's Day
flag appears on my uncle's grave, his wife is beside, beside
grandfather and grandmother's stone. Rough grass is mowed.

The loose stone cemetery edges are alive: red sugar maples,
white birch and pines. I read granite gravestones,
a three-hundred-year archive.

Shadows talk. Trees, like books, hold time.

Mission

Not a black cloaked devil
taking you piece by piece
in the chess game

rather, a primitive beast
wall-eyed, simple
with a strong sense of smell.

Sometimes a foolish
distraction delays it,

until the hunger sets in.

Tremor

He repairs the rusted latch on my cabin door.

He places six stones in the glossy flow of the
dwindling river so I can listen.

Water tumbles and curls.

Dangling leaves stir. My tree swing is veiled
by the weeping willow.

By autumn, yellow leaves in-fill the echoing spaces.
In due course the river is empty.

In the city, sparkling wine flows with music.
My blue dance dress is silk. The hem ripples.

I look back to see a man stand by the riverbed.

If you asked me what has become of the man,
I'd tell you I don't even remember his name.

I have forgotten the swing by the lyrical river.

I have forgotten the languorous summer.

Why do tremors remain?

A Thing with Feathers

—Emily Dickinson

Captured, carried in a purse, sold for a twenty.
My cage is set next to a cash register.
I'm labeled Amazon Double Yellow Head.
My breed smiles where our beak halves meet.
Our wide-eyed gaze fixes and beguiles.
The pet store owner proffers
Some say they live to be a hundred.

Two hundred dollars later, I am Miller
(named after Henry).

In time I molt my first wing feather,
crane my head down to retrieve it.
Place it in her hand. Luminescent.
She lightly taps my beak with her fingernail.
She has seen me tear quickly into things
exert three hundred pounds of pressure.
Riding on her shoulder, I lightly preen her ear.

I squawk if I'm left in the kitchen when company
comes. I do embarrass her with my chuckling
heh, heh, heh when I hear her manneristic laugh.
We share a voice. My first words: a honeyed
Hello Miller. I hear it every time she comes home.
I softly repeat it when I'm left alone looking out
the window. I add a robin's trill. I once cawed crow.

Weekends we play. Happy mornings I climb up to her
bed, am flipped on my back, given a ping pong ball
to juggle. I twirl it with my feet and never let it fall.
I learned that I could pick up a spoon with one foot,
hold it level for a treat. I like to waddle to the closet
with the mirrored door. I fluff and lunge
at the competition in the glass.

When I step up on her wrist, the rival bird
is vanquished, out of my sight.

Sometimes I perch on her forefinger, her thumb
clamped on my two front toes.
She whirls her arm to let me flap my wings.
She never would clip them. She likes to
press her ear against my chest to hear
the whirr of my two chambers.
She has two hearts.

Outside, I ride her wrist. One end of a rawhide
lace tied to my leg, one end to her finger.

And so, it was one jungle-humid day the walnut
tree above us filled with wild parrots come to roost,
a cacophony of African and Amazon like me, some
escaped, some born free. Raucous squawks, song bird
calls, words like *Hi honey, stop it, Kirk Kirk Kirk,*
Japanese and Spanish, a clear coloratura.
She is amused, but I already feel among them.

I crane my neck, aim an upturned eye,
then look at her and she at me.
I shift my weight to one leg,
quickly beak the tie undone (I must have
always known how). It dangles from her finger.
I tilt my head again. Look up to the restless tree.
She strokes my soft breast feathers.

Then her hand slowly rises. She whirls her arm
without clamped thumb. I lift.   We let go.

Bolete

Out of primal mesh
part of me rises
to be eaten.

Each Spring you search
the forest floor,
seek my fruiting body.

Hesitant footsteps pause
above my shady sanctum.
A knee is pressed

into the forest duff.
A forefinger and thumb
lift my barely open lid.

Once again, break me loose.
Your skin and filtered sun
warm my flesh.

You cup me in both hands,
inhale my musky scent.
I speak through it.

I offer the delectable.
Urge the ancient ritual.
Become earth, like me.

Clay

Short thick fingers push into a lump of clay. Next day
it hardens into a vessel. Sun says fire. The woman grunts.

Culture is born and there is stew.

Today a potter eats her to-go lunch by the lake.
She scoops up mud between reeds, avoiding the algae.

In the parking lot, she scrapes up dry dirt between the cracks,
avoiding cigarette butts.

She thinks in clay.

She bows her head, places her hands around the clay
not unlike praying—or scrubbing soil from home-grown potatoes.

Her studio is a brown kitchen—table, deep sink, tools almost
like those used for cooking. A large kiln huffs, ready for firing.

Earth, water, air and fire.

She loves the smell of earth like others do the scent
of baking bread.

She takes sherds from past miscalculations, grinds and kneads
them into the clay body.

Repurposed work can temper, bestow resilience.

Archeologists find perfect bowls with broken bottoms
that freed the vessels' spirit, or perhaps sacrificed beauty or labor.

Clay says whirl me on this wheel with intuition, touch me with
passion, cradle each curve.

Mud is alive.

Grit

This gritty desert roadway dips and twists.
Gravel shoulders trap the rain and burst in bloom
on poison slag and buckled beams and rust.
A mine fails. Coughs and calls and steel are still.

A worn sad house stands by abandoned track,
emits a deep low moan through stifling heat.
An acrid scent prevails. I peer into a room
through shredded curtains sewn with care.

Startled pigeons clamor for escape,
stream through broken windowpanes,
rise in swirls as in San Marco Square then fade—
another false storm desert cloud.

Bird droppings mound on stove and broken chair,
white layers spatter pans and checkered floor.
A saggy bed is propped against a battered door
beside a manly shoe and lady's small red party pair.

Perhaps they ate their breakfast that last day.
Were free from memories with no need to pack.
Perhaps they saw this cactus lit with feisty spines
and felt a breath of breeze behind their backs.

Garden Snake

I gift my skin
        gray lace, stripes, and stipples, light as the silk
    around the crown of your familiar garden hat.

How rapidly you pick it up.

My cabled body slips away in slow gear motion
        secretes wet straw mulch
    follows musky furrows.

You carry my gift with two hands to your writing room.
        Pity tiny tears, study mask and taper.
    Place it over sheaves of your dark work.

Think how good to be renewed.
        Shed old skin whole.
    Leave past ghosts to gravel.

A Breath of Will

—Emerson

Poppies re-seed in the driveway gravel,
purple petals nod on wiry stems.

Raw edges of cherries are halved by the birds;
the tree is both mine and theirs.

Last year there were only apples and plums.
I thin the green peaches so branches won't break

and string electrified fencing.

The bear rips the limbs, or I'd share
the fruit with her. For now, she licks ants,

dislodging large rocks in the woods.
Some are steps to scale the steep hill.

If I came face to face with her hunger, our fear—
fluttering shirt, ruffled up fur—

I would need to stand still, pretend to be big.

O breath of will, let me fit in.

Encounter

I step outside
to mix the stars
deep in my mind
for dreaming.

Across
the silent courtyard
wild sunflowers
startle me.

A tall tight group
stopped at the pavement,
pale in the flooded
window light.

Worn drooped leaves.
Bent petal heads
compel dark eyes
into my blue ones.

Then I too catch
the lurking scent of
autumn in the windless
August night.

Quickened weeks.
Hard freeze.

Crow Familiar

Crow cacophony.
black sky spirals
unknown

there is no denying
my lost spirit-lifter
a hunger I can't feed.

We once shared views.
I seek
what can be different

I take my crow
my wild familiar
my sad feather cache

fresh kill? intruder?
song dog? hawk?
crow confusion

suddenly a silent sky
tail, head, wing shafts-
four-ray stars

then I too spy
the glint of gloss
in matt gold leaves

fold and fall
crows like cinders
catch in limbs

Once we knew each other
this last fibrillation
leaves an empty chamber

When time in time
unwinds my crow
I'll make a flute

breath-less corridor
behind the beak
black frozen cry

carve spaced holes
blow breath
through a hollow bone.

Clawed toes grip-less
rumpled feathers
touched

play *diminuendo* with
whap/whap/woof of wingbeats
to shadows whirled on mine.

Sacred Datura

Against the canyon wall
radiating day heat into night
thorn-apple-devil, witch-weed

datura buds unfurl.
Beneath toothed leaves
white horns splay.

Fragrant moon-glow petals
draw the hawk moth pollinator.
Angel trumpets,

but what angel
heralds in the vision quest
pathways only known to shamans?

They lead the search within,
lend courage for the rite of passage
between delirium and death,

face the great motherless amnesia.
Dare to forget her and
purify for a new beginning.

Quest to know one's animal,
dare one's ghosts,
be sorcerer, break old hexes—fly.

Every spirit-wish and fear confronted.

As If I Would Forget

A murder of crows assail the rare Buteo Regalis
      solitary hawk, but for this agitation.

It emits an unfamiliar melancholy whistle
         veers and banks between hillside and sun.

Oscillating light pierces long slim wings
    Fra Angelico's pale idea of angel.

Suddenly, without wing beat Regalis slices
    through the cloudless sky until a

        dot.

That night a meteor at light-year's end
    cuts a burning arc into the hill.

Kairos

Daylight slants and stars have veered according to the season.

What am I but autumn passing? I face late sun, enjoy the warmth.
Know my long shadow drops behind.

A troubadour twangs: *Leaving you was easier—*
I lower the volume. My posture shifts in the pond-side chair.

Few find passion in the crowded years of toiling at a job.

Old age comes with force and fascination.
It asks us to give meaning to where we are.

I hear parting wingbeats across the pond. I see others join
        above the river, woods and fields.

If you asked me for the cost of life I've given to be with this land

I'd tell you I lived long enough.

        The price of stewardship was fair.

The Scale of Things

I dream Saturn rolls toward me, rock and ice rings
wheeling like birds. Cassini launches to explore new worlds.

The Titan lifts through fiery clouds. In minutes the rocket
gains over six thousand miles per hour.

Across Canaveral soft voices chorus *God Bless America: spacious
skies, God shed his light*—hymn to the wonderous mission.

Song drifts toward the silent bunker. The shamanistic mission team
listens.

Cassini will loop the ringed giant like hundreds of strands on a
yarn ball. Science for some, new geographies for all to see.

Mother once drove a Saturn, then a Subaru with the Pleiades
imprinted on the back.

We create constellations from points of light, make
stories from stars, create meaning to reckon vastness.

Between eons, nebula mesh like clouds of snow, stars
and space fold into each other. Our galaxy expands.

Within space-time we are multiple selves. Like Duchamp's
Nude Descending a Staircase—gender, ethnicity, age disappear.

We are stardust in motion.

Wind and Tree and Me

April 3, a flare high in the Palo Verde
little flame circle flower.
          Oh!
just now frayed away.
The wind is clocked at forty-three
miles an hour.

BB size buds are like bulbs
on Lilliputian Christmas trees.
By noon three yellow buds burst.
Desert flowers bloom quick
as the flick of a rattlesnake's tongue.
Then are done.

Branches list southwest.
I keep a list of wind speeds.
Between patio trees
the harsh Chihuahuan desert,
arroyo gouged plains,
jagged peaks, lava spew.

On the ridge sunlight turns
the jump-rope powerlines white
Do they whistle in the wind?
Beyond them contrails—
multiple streaks dissolve
in this blue-blown sky.

A gust through my feathery shade
tips over the patio chairs. Three blue
flower pillows are torn from
their moorings, skip through the air
to lodge in white thorn acacia.
I'm winded from the chase.

Wind taunts: a dangle, a tease
dares me retrieve my cushions.

I could purchase others,
but for months I would still see
blue shredded ghosts
flapping at me.

In this desert of infinite browns
(isn't all earth brown under our stuff?)
If ground shows, something grows.
I'm awed that everything barbed
survives being eaten, bitten or gnawed.
Yet another windy April 3.

Today I shall wear lime green. I'm
old but as intense as bark on my Verde tree.
                    Oh!
a yellow petal catches in my gray blown hair.

My home is Chihuahuan desert—

            you'll find me still, or still here.

About the Author

Linda Malm was published as a teen and only returned to poetry after she retired as a college dean. She was awarded a position as Writer of Los Luceros (the Robert Redford/NM Film Board enterprise). Her poetry has appeared in several issues of *Howl*, and the four *Adobe Walls* anthologies, as well as the *Iowa Summer Writing Festival Anthology, The Examined Life, Sugar Mule, Ishaan Literary Review, Ms. Aligned 4, Smoky Blue, Abandoned Mine, First Literary Review—East, Ube Issue 5, Waywords #9, The Taos Journal of Poetry #13*.

www.ingramcontent.com/pod-product-compliance
Lightning Source LLC
Chambersburg PA
CBHW030815090426
42737CB00010B/1278